C000182841

ROYAL COL

The Royal Court Theatre presents
the Northern Firebrand production of

SCARBOROUGH

by **Fiona Evans**

First performance at Apartment, Collingwood Street, Newcastle on 24 October 2006.
First performance at The Assembly Rooms, George Street, Edinburgh on 3 August 2007.
First performance of a revised production at Royal Court Jerwood Theatre Upstairs,
Sloane Square, London on 7 February 2008.

supported by

JERWOOD
NEW PLAYWRIGHTS

SCARBOROUGH
by **Fiona Evans**

Cast in order of appearance
Lauren **Holly Atkins**
Daz **Jack O'Connell**
Aiden **Daniel Mays**
Beth **Rebecca Ryan**

Director **Deborah Bruce**
Producer **Justine Watson**
Designer **Jo Newberry**
Assistant Director **Adaora Nwandu**∗
Casting Director **Amy Ball**
Production Manager **Sue Bird**
Stage Managers, **Carla Archer, Susie Jenkins**
Costume Supervisor **Jackie Orton**
Set Built by **100% Scenery Ltd.**

∗ The assistant director post is kindly supported by the Links of London Young Directors' Scheme.

The Royal Court and Stage Management wish to thank Sony Computer Entertainment for the kind loan of the PSP Portable.

2 – 31 May

ROYAL COURT

oxford street

by David Levi Addai

Director **Dawn Walton**

OXF
STR
W1

Tickets £15, £10 concs
020 7565 5000
www.royalcourttheatre.com

supported by

JERWOOD
NEW PLAYWRIGHTS

THE COMPANY

FIONA EVANS (writer)

THEATRE INCLUDES: Deepcut (in development); Scarborough (Edinburgh Festival Fringe); We Love You Arthur (Edinburgh Festival Fringe/tour); The Virgin of Stratford.

AWARDS INCLUDE: Fringe First 2007 for Scarborough.

Fiona has just completed the BBC Writers Academy 2007; she will be working on Doctors, EastEnders, Holby City and Casualty over the coming year.

HOLLY ATKINS (Lauren)

THEATRE INCLUDES: Scarborough (Edinburgh Festival Fringe); Summer Begins (Southwark Playhouse); One Flew Over the Cuckoo's Nest (Centreline/tour).

TELEVISION INCLUDES: Criminal Justice, The Sarah Jane Adventures, City Lights, Doctors, The Bill, Where the Heart Is, Casualty, The Project, Residents, Kiss Me Kate, EastEnders.

DEBORAH BRUCE (director)

FOR THE ROYAL COURT: Made of Stone.

THEATRE INCLUDES: Scarborough (Edinburgh Festival Fringe); Blame (Arcola/tour); My Own Show (Stephen Joseph Theatre); The Unexpected Man, In Praise of Love (Theatre Royal, Bath); Musik (Oxford Stage Co.); Taking Sides (No.1 tour); Death and the Ploughman (Gate, Notting Hill); Mrs Warren's Profession (Bristol Old Vic); Behsharam (Soho/Birmingham Rep.); The Woman Who Swallowed a Pin (Southwark Playhouse); Making Noise Quietly (Oxford Stage Co./Whitehall Theatre/tour); The Asylum Project (Riverside); The Inheritor (NT Studio); Romeo and Juliet (Chester Gateway); The Glass Menagerie, Our Country's Good, My Sister in this House, Hello and Goodbye, Oleanna (Theatr Clwyd).

DANIEL MAYS (Aiden)

FOR THE ROYAL COURT: Motortown, The Winterling, Ladybird, The One with the Oven, Just a Bloke.

OTHER THEATRE INCLUDES: M.A.D. (Bush).

TELEVISION INCLUDES: White Girl, Half Broken Things, Great News, Saddam's Tribe, Consent, Funland, Class of '76, Top Buzzer, Beneath the Skin, Keen Eddie, Tipping the Velvet, Bodily Harm, NCS, Dead Casual, Manchild, In Deep, EastEnders, The Bill.

FILM INCLUDES: Mr Nobody, Hippie Hippie Shake, Shifty, The Bank Job, Atonement, Middletown, A Good Year, Secret Life of Words, Vera Drake, Best Man, Rehab, All or Nothing, Pearl Harbor.

AWARDS INCLUDE: Palmare-Reims Television Festival 2004 – Best Actor (for Rehab).

JO NEWBERRY (designer)

This is Jo's first design for theatre.

FILM INCLUDES: Mrs Buchan, An Egg's an Egg, Wasps, Dance for a Stranger, Going, Look, Bait.

AS ART DIRECTOR, FILM AND TELEVISION INCLUDES: The Cottage, Heartbeat, My Parents are Aliens, School for Seduction, The Arc, Emmerdale, Where the Heart Is, Crossroads, Peak Practice, Brookside, Hollyoaks, Touch of Frost, Nasty Neighbours.

ADAORA NWANDU (assistant director)

THEATRE INCLUDES: African Odes (Soho).

FILM INCLUDES: Rag Tag, The Interns, Lay to Rest.

JACK O'CONNELL (Daz)

THEATRE INCLUDES: The Spider Man, Just (NT Shell Connections); The Musicians (NT Shell Connections/Nottingham Playhouse).

TELEVISION INCLUDES: Wire in the Blood, Holby City, Waterloo Road, The Bill, Doctors.

FILM INCLUDES: Eden Lake, Black Dog, This is England.

REBECCA RYAN (Beth)

THEATRE INCLUDES: Tommy (M/CR Palace).

TELEVISION INCLUDES: Shameless, Holby City, State of Play, Emmerdale, Casualty.

FILM INCLUDES: The Draft.

RADIO INCLUDES: The Swimming Pool, Hush Little Baby.

24 April – 7 June

the city

by Martin Crimp

Director **Katie Mitchell**
Designer **Vicki Mortimer**
Lighting **Paule Constable**
Sound **Gareth Fry**

Tickets £10, £15, £25
020 7565 5000
www.royalcourttheatre.com

THE ENGLISH STAGE COMPANY
AT THE ROYAL COURT

'For me the theatre is really a religion or way of life. You must decide what you feel the world is about and what you want to say about it, so that everything in the theatre you work in is saying the same thing ...
A theatre must have a recognisable attitude. It will have one, whether you like it or not.'

George Devine, first artistic director of the English Stage Company: notes for an unwritten book.

photo: Stephen Cummiskey

The Royal Court Theatre in London's Sloane Square has presented some of the most influential plays in modern theatre history. At the turn of the twentieth century, the Royal Court was under the direction of Harley Granville-Barker and staged plays by Ibsen, Galsworthy, Yeats, Maeterlinck and Shaw. In 1956 George Devine became the first Artistic Director of the English Stage Company at the Royal Court. His intention was to create an international theatre of experiment that was devoted to the discovery of the future in playwriting. The production of John Osborne's Look Back in Anger in 1956 ushered in a new generation of playwrights, directors, actors and designers who together established the Court as the first theatre in London that prioritised the work of contemporary playwrights. Among them were Arnold Wesker, Ann Jellicoe, Edward Bond, John Arden, Christopher Hampton and David Storey. New plays were programmed alongside classics, and the company was from its earliest days committed to producing the best new international plays, including those of Ionesco, Genet and Beckett.
In 1969 the Royal Court opened the first second space in a British theatre; the Jerwood Theatre Upstairs has been a site for radical experimentation and has introduced audiences to some of the most influential new voices of the last 40 years, including Wole Soyinka, Caryl Churchill, David Hare, Howard Brenton, Howard Barker, Peter Gill, Martin Crimp, Sam Shepard and Jim Cartwright. Many outstanding young playwrights have established their careers here; among them Joe Penhall, Sarah Kane, Roy Williams, Rebecca Prichard, Mark Ravenhill, Martin McDonagh, Conor McPherson, Simon Stephens and debbie tucker green.

The Royal Court's Artistic Programme is only partially about the work seen on its stages. Many of its resources, and indeed the roots of the organisation, are devoted to the discovery and nurturing of new writers and the development of new plays. The Royal Court is in the business of asking questions about the world we live in and about what a play itself can be. The theatre's aim is to support both emerging and established writers in exploring new territory.

The Royal Court's long and successful history of innovation has been built by generations of gifted and imaginative individuals. For information on the many ways you can help support the theatre, please contact the Development Department on 020 7565 5079.

NORTHERN FIREBRAND

Founded in 2004 by Fiona Evans, Newcastle-based Northern Firebrand launched with a North East tour of Kathleen McCreery's Flight Paths. The following year the company began their on-going association with New Writing North, with Evans's play We Love You Arthur at the Edinburgh Festival Fringe. Deborah Bruce and Justine Watson joined Northern Firebrand in 2007. In the same year, the company returned to the Fringe with the award-winning Scarborough and are thrilled to present this new production of the play at The Royal Court in 2008.

Scarborough was originally commissioned by New Writing North as part of the Orange Bitesize Theatre Programme 2006. Daz was played by James Baxter and Lauren was played by Ashlea Sanderson.

Northern Firebrand are committed to producing exciting and innovative theatre from the North East.

Northern Firebrand gratefully acknowledges the support of New Writing North and The Empty Space.

For their support of Scarborough, we would also like to give particular thanks to everyone at the Royal Court, as well as: Arts and Business North East, James Baxter, Alex Black, Lesley Bruce, Beth Bryson, William Burdett-Coutts, Steve Chambers, Richard Clarke at Project North East, Rory Coulson, Julia Crampsie, Bridget Deane, Anna Disley, Barrie Dunn, David Lee, John Lloyd Fillingham, Duncan Fisher, Nick Hern, Jeremy Herrin, Debbie Horsfield, Johannes Kratzsch, Brian Lonsdale, Claire Malcolm, Keith Pattison, Natalie Querol, Kathleen & Ray Richardson, Caroline Routh, Ashlea Sanderson, Mary Shields, Liz Smith, Ian Sterling, Lucy Taylor and Joseph White.

northern
FIREBRAND

For more information about Northern Firebrand or Scarborough please contact Justine Watson at info@northernfirebrand.co.uk

JERWOOD
NEW PLAYWRIGHTS

Since 1994 Jerwood New Playwrights has contributed to 54 new plays at the Royal Court including Joe Penhall's SOME VOICES, Mark Ravenhill's SHOPPING AND FUCKING (co-production with Out of Joint), Ayub Khan Din's EAST IS EAST (co-production with Tamasha), Martin McDonagh's THE BEAUTY QUEEN OF LEENANE (co-production with Druid Theatre Company), Conor McPherson's THE WEIR, Nick Grosso's REAL CLASSY AFFAIR, Sarah Kane's 4.48 PSYCHOSIS, Gary Mitchell's THE FORCE OF CHANGE, David Eldridge's UNDER THE BLUE SKY, David Harrower's PRESENCE, Simon Stephens' HERONS, Roy Williams' CLUBLAND, Leo Butler's REDUNDANT, Michael Wynne's THE PEOPLE ARE FRIENDLY, David Greig's OUTLYING ISLANDS, Zinnie Harris' NIGHTINGALE AND CHASE, Grae Cleugh's FUCKING GAMES, Rona Munro's IRON, Richard Bean's UNDER THE WHALEBACK, Ché Walker's FLESH WOUND, Roy Williams' FALLOUT, Mick Mahoney's FOOD CHAIN, Ayub Khan Din's NOTES ON FALLING LEAVES, Leo Butler's LUCKY DOG, Simon Stephens' COUNTRY MUSIC, Laura Wade's BREATHING CORPSES, Debbie Tucker Green's STONING MARY, David Eldridge's INCOMPLETE AND RANDOM ACTS OF KINDNESS, Gregory Burke's ON TOUR, Stella Feehily's O GO MY MAN, Simon Stephens' MOTORTOWN, Simon Farquhar's RAINBOW KISS and April de Angelis, Stella Feehily, Tanika Gupta, Chloe Moss and Laura Wade's CATCH.

In 2007 Jerwood New Playwrights supported MY CHILD by Mike Bartlett and THAT FACE by Polly Stenham, for which she won the TMA and Evening Standard Awards for Most Promising Playwright.

The Jerwood Charitable Foundation is a registered charity dedicated to imaginative and responsible funding of the arts and other areas of human endeavour and excellence.

Mike Bartlett's MY CHILD
(photo: Keith Pattison)

Polly Stenham's THAT FACE
(photo: John Haynes)

PROGRAMME SUPPORTERS

The Royal Court (English Stage Company Ltd) receives its principal funding from Arts Council England, London. It is also supported financially by a wide range of private companies, charitable and public bodies, and earns the remainder of its income from the box office and its own trading activities.

The Genesis Foundation supports the Royal Court's work with International Playwrights.

The Jerwood Charitable Foundation supports new plays by new playwrights through the Jerwood New Playwrights series.

The Artistic Director's Chair is supported by a lead grant from The Peter Jay Sharp Foundation, contributing to the activities of the Artistic Director's office. Over the past ten years the BBC has supported the Gerald Chapman Fund for directors.

ROYAL COURT DEVELOPMENT BOARD
John Ayton
Anthony Burton
Sindy Caplan (Vice-Chair)
Cas Donald
Allie Esiri
AC Farstad
Celeste Fenichel
Emma Marsh
Mark Robinson
William Russell (Chair)

PUBLIC FUNDING
Arts Council England, London
British Council
London Challenge
Royal Borough of Kensington & Chelsea

CHARITABLE DONATIONS
American Friends of the Royal Court Theatre
Bulldog Prinsep Theatrical Fund
Gerald Chapman Fund
Columbia Foundation
The Sidney & Elizabeth Corob Charitable Trust
Cowley Charitable Trust
The Dorset Foundation
The D'oyly Carte Charitable Trust
E*TRADE Financial
The Edwin Fox Foundation
Francis Finlay
The Garfield Weston Foundation
Genesis Foundation
Haberdashers' Company
Jerwood Charitable Foundation
John Thaw Foundation

Lloyds TSB Foundation for England and Wales
Dorothy Loudon Foundation
Lynn Foundation
John Lyon's Charity
The Magowan Family Foundation
The Laura Pels Foundation
The Martin Bowley Charitable Trust
Paul Hamlyn Foundation
The Peggy Ramsay Foundation
Quercus Charitable Trust
Rose Foundation
Royal College of Psychiatrists
The Royal Victoria Hall Foundation
The Peter Jay Sharp Foundation
Sobell Foundation
Wates Foundation

SPONSORS
Arts & Business
BBC
Coutts & Co
Dom Perignon
Kudos Film and Television
Links of London
Pemberton Greenish
Smythson of Bond Street

BUSINESS BENEFACTORS & MEMBERS
Grey London
Hugo Boss
Lazard
Merrill Lynch
Tiffany & Co.
Vanity Fair

INDIVIDUAL SUPPORTERS
ICE-BREAKERS
Anonymous
Jane Attias
Ossi and Paul Burger
Mrs Helena Butler
Cynthia Corbett
Shantelle David
Kim Dunn
Charlotte & Nick Fraser
David Lanch
Colette & Peter Levy
Watcyn Lewis
David Marks
Nicola McFarland
Janet & Michael Orr
Mr & Mrs William Poeton
Jenny Sheridan
Lois Sieff OBE
Gail Steele
Nick & Louise Steidl

GROUND-BREAKERS
Anonymous
Moira Andreae
John and Annoushka Ayton
Elizabeth & Adam Bandeen
Sindy & Jonathan Caplan
Mr & Mrs Gavin Casey
Carole & Neville Conrad
Andrew Cryer
Cas Donald
Robyn M Durie
Hugo Eddis
Tom & Simone Fenton
Ginny Finegold
Wendy Fisher
Tim Fosberry
Lydia & Manfred Gorvy
Richard & Maria Grand
Don & Sue Guiney

Sam & Caroline Haubold
The Hon Mrs George Iliffe
Nicholas Josefowitz
Jack and Linda Keenan
Peter & Maria Kellner
Varian Ayers and Gary Knisely
Rosanna Laurence
Kathryn Ludlow
Deborah & Stephen Marquardt
Emma Marsh
Duncan Matthews QC
Barbara Minto
Pat Morton
Gavin & Ann Neath
Kadee Robbins
Paul & Jill Ruddock
William & Hilary Russell
Ian & Carol Sellars
Brian D Smith
Sue Stapely
Carl & Martha Tack
Amanda Vail

BOUNDARY-BREAKERS
Katie Bradford
Edna & Peter Goldstein
Reade and Elizabeth Griffith
Jan and Michael Topham

MOVER-SHAKERS
John Garfield
Miles Morland

MAJOR DONORS
Daniel & Joanna Friel
NoraLee & Jon Sedmak

FOR THE ROYAL COURT

Royal Court Theatre, Sloane Square, London SW1W 8AS
Tel: 020 7565 5050 Fax: 020 7565 5001
info@royalcourttheatre.com, www.royalcourttheatre.com

Artistic Director **Dominic Cooke**
Associate Directors **Ramin Gray*, Sacha Wares+**
Artistic Associate **Emily McLaughlin**
Associate Producer **Diane Borger**
Trainee Associate Director **Lyndsey Turner‡**
Artistic Assistant **Rebecca Hanna-Grindall**

Literary Manager **Ruth Little**
Literary Associate **Terry Johnson***
Pearson Playwright **Mike Bartlett†**
Literary Assistant **Nicola Wass**

Associate Director International **Elyse Dodgson**
International Administrator **Chris James**
International Assistant **William Drew**

Associate Director YWP **Ola Animashawun**
YWP Administrator **Nina Lyndon**
Outreach Worker **Lucy Dunkerley**
Writers' Tutor **Leo Butler***

Casting Director **Amy Ball**
Casting Assistant **Lucy Taylor**

Head of Production **Paul Handley**
JTU Production Manager **Sue Bird**
Production Assistant **Sarah Davies**
Head of Lighting **Matt Drury**
Lighting Deputy **Nicki Brown**
Lighting Assistant **Stephen Andrews**
Lighting Board Operator **Joe Hicks**
Head of Stage **Steven Stickler**
Stage Deputy **Duncan Russell**
Stage Chargehand **Lee Crimmen**
Chargehand Carpenter **Richard Martin**
Head of Sound **Ian Dickinson**
Sound Deputy **David McSeveney**
Sound Operator **Mark Cunningham**
Head of Costume **Iona Kenrick**
Costume Deputy **Jackie Orton**
Wardrobe Assistant **Pam Anson**

Executive Director **Kate Horton**
Administrator **Oliver Rance**
Head of Finance **Helen Perryer**
Finance Manager **Silethemba Ncube***
Senior Finance Officer **Martin Wheeler**
Finance Officer **Rachel Harrison***

Head of Communications **Kym Bartlett**
Marketing Manager **Kelly Duffy**
Press Officer **Stephen Pidcock**
Audience Development Officer **Gemma Frayne**
Audience Development Assistant **Susannah Ostrom**
Press Intern **Ruth Hawkins**

Sales Manager **David Kantounas**
Deputy Sales Manager **Stuart Grey**
Box Office Sales Assistants **Daniel Alicandro,
Fiona Clift, Shane Hough, Rebecca Ryan**

Head of Development **Jenny Mercer**
Development Manager Individual Giving **Hannah Clifford**
Development Manager Corporate **Skye Crawford**
Development Assistant **Lucy James**

Theatre Manager **Bobbie Stokes**
Front of House Manager **Lucinda Springett**
Duty Manager **Claire Simpson**
Bar and Food Manager **Darren Elliott**
Bookshop Manager **Simon David**
Assistant Bookshop Manager **Edin Suljic***
Building Maintenance Administrator **Jon Hunter**
Stage Door/Reception **Simon David*,
Paul Lovegrove, Tyrone Lucas, David Zezulka***

Thanks to all of our box office assistants, ushers and Café Bar staff.

+ Sacha Wares' post is supported by the BBC through the
Gerald Chapman Fund.

‡ The Trainee Associate Director Bursary is supported by the
Quercus Trust.

† This theatre has the support of the Pearson Playwrights' scheme,
sponsored by the Peggy Ramsay Foundation.

* Part-time.

SCARBOROUGH

Fiona Evans

For Deborah

Scarborough is as much yours as it is mine.

Follow your heart.

Characters

DAZ, *15 years old*
LAUREN, *29 years old*
AIDEN, *29 years old*
BETH, *15 years old*

The play takes place in a double room in a Scarborough bed and breakfast.

Special thanks is reserved for Justine Watson, 'Our Kath' and Bridget Deane; without whose hard work, support and friendship this play would never have made it to Edinburgh or the Royal Court.

F. E.

This text went to press before the end of rehearsals and so may differ slightly from the play as performed.

PART ONE

Scene One

Sunday.

DAZ *and* LAUREN *sit with their backs to each other on the edge of the bed, the air is heavy.*

LAUREN. I've always hated Sundays…

DAZ. Me too…

LAUREN. That sick feeling, that…

DAZ. I haven't done me homework…

LAUREN. Feeling. The end of…

DAZ. I can't believe this is it…

LAUREN. Over before it's…

DAZ. Game over.

LAUREN. Begun.

DAZ. We should have –

LAUREN. Swum against the tide.

DAZ (*beat*). I can't swim.

LAUREN. But you… you lied.

DAZ. You're the liar, I just can't crawl.

LAUREN. I would have taught you, I would have…

DAZ. Thrown me in the deep end.

LAUREN. Saved you.

DAZ. I need some air… this room…

LAUREN. It's changed.

DAZ. We've… I need to get out.

LAUREN. Calm…

DAZ. I'm sick of talking.

LAUREN. Hold on…

DAZ. Every man for himself.

I want to go home.

LAUREN. I need to know…

DAZ. You think I'd tell? Your secret's safe with me – memory deleted.

LAUREN. Memory deleted.

Lights fade.

Scene Two

Friday.

A single red rose stands in an improvised vase – a plastic bottle. Next to it sits a cheap teddy bear clutching a heart on which 'I love Scarborough' is written. An iPod blares music. DAZ and LAUREN get ready to hit the town. They drink alcopops.

DAZ. Lock up your daughters, Daz is in town.

LAUREN. Shall we go to the same place as before?

DAZ. Let's try somewhere on the front.

LAUREN. It's a bit tacky.

DAZ. I'll show you tacky.

DAZ *gets out his phone and starts to show her photos of their last visit.*

LAUREN. Look at the state of me.

DAZ. You look great.

LAUREN. With candyfloss all over my face? I'd forgotten about those hats.

DAZ. I've still got mine.

LAUREN. I told you it rained that day.

DAZ. It was just a few clouds. Anyway – (*He starts to make a move.*) the last thing on my mind's the weather.

LAUREN. Again? We've got all weekend for that.

DAZ. Get in.

LAUREN. I'm sure the landlady suspects…

DAZ. Nosy cow. (*Beat.*) I'll give her something to gossip about.

DAZ *bounces on the bed, making it creak, as if having sex.*

LAUREN. Stop it.

DAZ. I'm a naughty boy, spank me –

LAUREN. Daz!

LAUREN *dives on him, trying to stop the noise, she holds her hand across his mouth. DAZ is trying to say something but she can't make it out.*

Promise you won't shout.

DAZ. Mmm-mmm.

She removes her hand.

You're smothering me.

LAUREN. Are you saying I'm fat?

DAZ. Cuddly.

LAUREN. I'll have you know I was regional under-eighteens swimming champion.

DAZ. That was a while ago.

LAUREN. You cheeky bastard.

DAZ. Joke, joke.

LAUREN. Not funny.

DAZ. You're not fat.

Beat. LAUREN *is still huffed.*

You're not fucking fat.

Trying a different tactic, DAZ *picks up the bear and starts talking to her through it.*

What are you doing, Mammy?

LAUREN *looks at him, she is playing unimpressed.*

Are you in a huff? Daz says he's really sorry.

LAUREN. Well, tell Daz, if he's really sorry he could tidy up his mess and unpack the rest of his stuff before we go out.

DAZ. Daz says that's boring.

LAUREN. Life can be boring.

DAZ. You look… mm-mmm… very sexy.

LAUREN. Do you think it's too much?

DAZ. Yes. It's great. The more chest the better, I want to show you off to the world.

LAUREN. I need the…

She indicates to the bathroom.

DAZ. Again?

LAUREN. It's those alcopops.

LAUREN *exits to the bathroom.* DAZ *admires himself in the mirror, tests his breath against his hand.*

DAZ (*to* LAUREN). Oh my God, it's happened again.

LAUREN (*offstage*). What?

DAZ. Every time I look in the mirror, I get better looking. (*To* LAUREN.) Hurry up… (*To himself.*) You lucky lady… (*To* LAUREN.) Ha'way man, Lauren…

She enters.

LAUREN. I can't do it.

DAZ. Do what?

LAUREN. I can't go out…

DAZ. Are you okay?

LAUREN. Not really.

DAZ. Are you sick?

LAUREN. Sort of.

DAZ. It must be the WKD, I got them cheap from the dodgy offy, I bet they were out of date.

LAUREN. It's not the drink.

DAZ. What then?

LAUREN. Someone might see us.

DAZ. Lauren, lots of people are going to see us.

LAUREN. Exactly.

DAZ. But they don't know who we are. They don't know…

LAUREN. I know.

DAZ. So we'll steer clear of mind-readers.

LAUREN. I'm being serious. Anyone could see us.

DAZ. We're not exactly the Beckhams, I don't think we're being tailed by the Geordie paparazzi.

LAUREN. I'm not going out.

DAZ. Lauren, man.

LAUREN. I'm sorry, it's just…

DAZ. It's me birthday tomorrow, we can't stay in all weekend.

LAUREN. I can't do it.

DAZ. It didn't bother you last time.

LAUREN. That was just a day trip.

DAZ. We played on the arcades, we went swimming.

LAUREN. I went swimming.

DAZ. I forgot my kit. (*Beat.*) We even kissed in public.

LAUREN. It was dark.

DAZ. Don't bullshit me, Lauren.

LAUREN. I'm the one taking all the risks. If we get found out…

DAZ. We won't…

LAUREN. It's my life on the line. It's my…

DAZ. Okay, okay, we'll stay in.

LAUREN. Thanks. (*Beat.*) I've got something that might cheer you up.

She gets out his card and two presents, hiding the larger one.

DAZ. It's not until tomorrow.

LAUREN. So!

DAZ starts to open the smaller present unenthusiastically.

You're supposed to open the card first.

DAZ. So!

It's a game for a PSP.

I haven't got a PSP.

LAUREN reveals the larger present.

No way.

LAUREN. Way.

He tears at the wrapping. It's a PSP. Clearly delighted.

DAZ. Oh my God, this is the best present ever.

LAUREN. I'm glad you like it.

DAZ. I fucking love it.

He gives her a big kiss.

Can I put it on?

LAUREN. Not now.

DAZ. Wait till I tell Greavsie.

LAUREN. You can't say it was from me.

DAZ. I'm not stupid.

LAUREN. I know, I just panic sometimes.

DAZ. Well, you shouldn't.

LAUREN. I can't help it.

DAZ. I've got a present for you.

LAUREN. For me?

DAZ. To say thanks for this weekend.

LAUREN. You haven't opened your card yet.

DAZ. Close your eyes.

LAUREN. Do I have –

DAZ. Close them.

LAUREN *closes her eyes.* DAZ *takes out his school photo and puts it on the table.*

LAUREN. Can I open them?

DAZ. Count to three.

LAUREN. One, two, three. (*She opens her eyes.*) Is this some kind of joke?

DAZ. Do you not like it? Me mam says…

LAUREN. Daz, that's not the point. Where am I going to keep it?

DAZ. In your office.

LAUREN. At school?

DAZ. Unless you've got one somewhere else.

LAUREN. The same office I share with Mr Lynch? The same office I have tutorials in with your classmates?

DAZ. I hadn't thought about that.

LAUREN. No, Daz, you never do.

DAZ. Sorry.

LAUREN. I'm always the one thinking…

DAZ. Alright, man.

LAUREN. The one planning…

DAZ. I get your point.

LAUREN. The one organising.

DAZ. Stop it, man, you're doing me head in.

LAUREN. Keep your voice down.

DAZ (*sarcastically*). Are you frightened you might get found out? Frightened that the landlady might hear? (*Beat. Seriously.*) I'm not bothered who knows, I'm not ashamed…

LAUREN. I'm sorry, Darren. The photo's lovely, it's just…

DAZ. You could keep it in your drawer.

LAUREN. What would be the point?

DAZ. To look at.

LAUREN. I'm sick of hiding.

DAZ. Well, don't.

LAUREN. If anyone found out…

DAZ. I know, you could lose your job.

LAUREN. It's more serious than that. If the head, if anyone ever...

DAZ. They won't.

DAZ puts the photo back in his bag. LAUREN *smiles weakly.* DAZ *starts to kiss her.*

LAUREN. What do you think you're doing?

DAZ. You might as well take advantage while you still can, I'll be legal tomorrow.

Lights fade.

Scene Three

Saturday.

DAZ *enters with a bag of provisions, he is really agitated.*

LAUREN. What's the matter?

DAZ. I've got some really bad news.

LAUREN. Daz, what is it?

DAZ. I've just bumped into Mr Scott.

LAUREN (*beat, shocked*). The head?

DAZ. Walking down the street. What the fuck's he doing in Scarborough?

LAUREN. Did he see you?

DAZ. He said hello, wanted to know what I was doing here.

LAUREN. What did you say?

DAZ. I said I was here with friends. But the... the look he gave us.

LAUREN. What look? Like what? Do it.

DAZ. Like… (*He demonstrates*.) I was on my way out of the newsagent and there he was, I just froze. I said, 'Hello Sir', and he just… the look he gave us… he knows…

LAUREN. He doesn't know!

DAZ. I'm telling you…

LAUREN. He doesn't know. He can't.

DAZ. He must…

LAUREN. Shut up.

DAZ. He must know that I'm… (*Laughing*.) only joking.

The penny drops. LAUREN *doesn't know whether to laugh or cry.*

LAUREN. You fucking shit. You little shit.

LAUREN *is frustrated and embarrassed to have been taken in, but better this than the alternative.* DAZ *is creased up, glad to have some fun back in the relationship.*

Oh God.

DAZ. What would he be doing in Scarborough?

LAUREN. That is not funny.

DAZ. I'm really sorry.

LAUREN. It's so not funny.

He continues to laugh.

Daz! It's not fucking funny.

DAZ. Come here.

LAUREN. Get away.

DAZ. Okay, I'm really sorry.

LAUREN. You're not sorry.

DAZ. It was funny. It was… (*He cracks up laughing.*)

LAUREN. It's not funny.

He continues to laugh.

Darren!

DAZ. I'm sorry, I am sorry.

They both crack up.

Serious.

LAUREN. Oh God.

DAZ (*trying to be serious*). It's a great day out there – sun's shining, birds are singing.

LAUREN. Headmaster's on the prowl.

DAZ. You're not going to believe anything I ever say again, are you?

LAUREN. No.

DAZ. No.

LAUREN (*taking the piss*). Nah.

DAZ. Nah?

LAUREN (*emphatic*). Never.

DAZ. What if I said I loved you? (*Beat.*) Would you believe that?

LAUREN. Stop being stupid.

DAZ. I'm not being stupid.

LAUREN. Yes you are.

DAZ. Maybe I am, but it doesn't mean I'm lying.

LAUREN. Can we change the subject?

DAZ. Okay.

DAZ goes to the window.

I got you a paper.

She takes a copy of the Sun *out of the bag* DAZ *brought in. She looks disapproving.*

I wanted to read the football.

LAUREN. I get enough sport at school.

DAZ. Look at how fast those clouds are moving.

LAUREN. Yeah.

DAZ. Why do clouds sometimes move fast and sometimes they don't move at all?

LAUREN. I don't know.

DAZ. What's inside them?

LAUREN. Twenty questions!

DAZ. It must be something inside them, or…

LAUREN. The wind.

DAZ. Nah, too easy. Must be pressure, or atmosphere, or…

LAUREN. Why make it more complex than it is?

DAZ. Scientific gas? Or it could be the amount of rain inside.

LAUREN. I don't know.

DAZ. Well, you're the teacher.

LAUREN. PE teacher. You should take more notice in your geography class.

DAZ. Why would I want to listen to Mrs Robson when I can watch you warming up in the yard.

LAUREN. One hundred lines – I must not perv on my teacher.

DAZ. Doing your squat thrusts. I must have missed the introduction to clouds lesson.

LAUREN. Introduction to clouds. I'd like to introduce you to a cloud. Here's a cloud. Hello Mr Cloud.

DAZ. Tell me, why do you move so fast?

They fall about laughing.

LAUREN. I wish we could just stay here for ever.

They have a moment.

DAZ. What do you call the wife of a Scottish cloud?

LAUREN. I don't know, what do you call the wife of a Scottish cloud?

DAZ. Mrs McCloud. I made that up. Do you get it?

LAUREN. Yes.

LAUREN *picks up the* Sun, *there is a paedophile story on the front page.*

DAZ. What's up with you?

LAUREN. I can't believe you bought this shit.

DAZ. I don't know what you want.

DAZ *starts to read his magazine.*

LAUREN. Disgusting.

DAZ. You don't have to read it.

LAUREN. I'm talking about the little kid who was molested.

DAZ. Oh yeah – Pervert.

LAUREN. I mean, who could…

DAZ. Fuckin' beast, they should lock him up and throw away the key.

LAUREN. Yeah.

They read for a while.

DAZ. Have you ever thought of plastic surgery?

LAUREN. What are you saying?

DAZ. Just asking.

LAUREN. Do you think I need it?

DAZ. Loads of people are doing it.

LAUREN. You think I need it.

DAZ. Well…

LAUREN. Don't you?

He looks pointedly at her.

DAZ. A bit of enhancement wouldn't go amiss.

LAUREN. Fuck off.

DAZ. Got ya!

LAUREN. Grow up.

DAZ. You wouldn't fancy me then – Pervert!

LAUREN. Daz!

DAZ. Cradle-snatcher!

LAUREN. You bastard!

DAZ. Joke.

LAUREN. Not funny.

DAZ blows her a kiss.

You think you're so clever.

DAZ. I'm the teacher's pet.

Something catches DAZ's eye in the magazine, LAUREN's interest is pricked. She surreptitiously looks over her shoulder.

LAUREN. Like blondes, do you?

DAZ. Who doesn't?

LAUREN. Young ones?

DAZ. I'm sixteen.

DAZ's *phone beeps, he has a text. He laughs.*

LAUREN. What's the big joke?

DAZ. You wouldn't get it.

LAUREN. Is it from Sam?

DAZ. Sam?

LAUREN. Forgotten her already?

DAZ. I know who she is.

LAUREN. Did you buy her roses?

DAZ. No.

LAUREN. I bet you did. Have you got photos of her on your phone?

DAZ. No.

DAZ *puts the phone in his pocket – guilty as charged.*

LAUREN. Do you still see her?

DAZ. We're in the same year.

LAUREN. I meant…

DAZ. I know.

LAUREN. Well?

DAZ. Not really.

LAUREN. What's that supposed to mean?

DAZ. Why are you so interested?

LAUREN. I'm not.

DAZ. Well, can we drop it.

LAUREN. Please yourself.

DAZ. Hang on, you're not…

LAUREN. No!

DAZ. You are.

LAUREN. Don't be ridiculous.

DAZ. Jealous.

LAUREN. Of a fifteen-year-old?

DAZ. You've shagged one, why can't you be jealous of one?

Silence.

Anyway, you're the one with the boyfriend.

LAUREN. You're so immature.

DAZ. Er – yes. What did you expect? George fucking Clooney?

Long pause.

LAUREN. Do you ever think about the future?

DAZ. What, like flying cars?

LAUREN. I'm being serious.

DAZ. Me too, they'd be great. (*Beat.*) 'Course I think about the future. I want to get me A-levels and that, and maybe go to college, like you.

LAUREN. That's… great.

DAZ. I don't want to end up like my mam and dad.

LAUREN. Not all marriages are bad.

DAZ. How would you know?

LAUREN. Well, they can't be.

DAZ. Don't see the point of marriage.

LAUREN. Why?

DAZ. How many happily married couples do you know?

LAUREN. Lots.

DAZ. Name one.

LAUREN. What?

DAZ. Name one. 'Cos I don't know any.

LAUREN. That's because you're fifteen.

DAZ. Sixteen. Prove me wrong.

LAUREN. You're putting me on the spot.

DAZ. You said you knew loads.

LAUREN. Your mam and dad can't be that unhappy.

DAZ. Can't stand each other.

LAUREN. They're still together.

DAZ. He's a womanising bastard and she hates his guts.

LAUREN. Why don't they split up?

DAZ. I don't know.

LAUREN. I suppose people have their reasons.

DAZ. Stupid ones if you ask me. If you're that unhappy that you'd shag someone else, then why stay with the person in the first place?

LAUREN. Well, it's not as simple as –

DAZ. It's black and white as far as I'm concerned. He's a bastard. He can get away with it so he does. He doesn't respect her, how can he? If you don't have respect…

He realises the implication of what he has just said.

LAUREN. Then what's the point.

DAZ. Sorry, I…

LAUREN. Don't be.

DAZ. I meant what I said.

LAUREN. Apology accepted.

DAZ. When I said I loved you.

LAUREN. Daz.

DAZ. For real… (*Long pause*.) Do you love me?

Lights fade.

Scene Four

Sunday.

LAUREN *is in the bathroom, finishing off a call to Chris.*

LAUREN (*offstage*). Still hungover… I know, sorry, we've been busy… yes, I've thought about it… we'll talk when I get back… yes, I miss you… okay, babe, bye… love you too. (*Kisses into phone and ends call.*)

LAUREN *enters.*

You were up early.

DAZ. Couldn't sleep.

LAUREN. Where've you been?

DAZ. Walking.

LAUREN. Obviously.

DAZ. And thinking.

DAZ *picks up the PSP and starts playing.*

LAUREN. We need to talk.

DAZ. Shit.

LAUREN. Darren.

DAZ. Nearly got blasted.

LAUREN. Are you listening?

DAZ. Yes. Get in.

LAUREN. This is serious.

DAZ. I know, I'm onto my last life.

LAUREN. You've been playing all weekend.

DAZ. Fuck. Game over. Must try harder.

LAUREN. We need to talk.

DAZ. That's what they say in the films, when they're about to dump somebody.

LAUREN. Don't be unreasonable.

DAZ. Unreasonable? I couldn't get a word out of you last night. Now you want to talk, so we'll talk. Fire away.

LAUREN. It's not…

DAZ. Not what?

LAUREN. Well…

DAZ. The same?

LAUREN. Working. It's not…

DAZ. Funny that. It was working on Friday. 'Yes, Daz; more, Daz; I've never felt like this, Daz.'

LAUREN. I'm sorry, I thought…

DAZ. Come on, don't be shy, Miss Potts, what were you thinking? You bring me here for a dirty weekend, a birthday treat. Then you go all weird on me. Won't go out. I'd like to know what the fuck's going on 'cos this is doing my head in.

LAUREN. This is really difficult for me.

DAZ. Like Pythagoras.

LAUREN. I wish there was a formula.

DAZ. Formula. I'll give you a formula. Daz, plus Lauren, to the power of Chris, equals Daz is fucked.

LAUREN. Don't bring him into it.

DAZ. So it's okay for you to nag me about my ex all weekend, but I can't mention your boyfriend's name – cool.

LAUREN. I was out of order, I should never…

DAZ. What's he like?

LAUREN. Daz.

DAZ. It's an easy question.

LAUREN. I don't…

DAZ. Well, I do, what the fuck's he like? Is he like me? What's so funny?

LAUREN. Nothing.

DAZ. How old is he? He's young, isn't he? How old?

LAUREN. Forty –

DAZ (*incredulous*). Forty?

LAUREN. Seven.

DAZ. Forty-seven? (*Beat.*) Forty-fucking-seven!

He'll soon be dead.

LAUREN. It's not important.

DAZ. What? The age or him?

LAUREN. The age… him… both.

DAZ. Well, leave him.

LAUREN. What?

DAZ. If he's not important, then leave him.

LAUREN. That's not… It's not as simple as that.

DAZ. It is to me.

LAUREN. You don't understand.

DAZ. Because I'm just a kid?

LAUREN. I never said that.

DAZ. I'm old enough to shag, but not old enough to understand. Explain. Go on, you're the teacher.

LAUREN. I'm sorry, Daz.

DAZ. What for? For nagging? For taking me to bed? For being a selfish bitch?

LAUREN. Please.

DAZ. For breaking my…

LAUREN. Daz, don't…

DAZ. Don't tell me what to do, we're not in school now.

LAUREN. I know how you must be feeling.

DAZ. Do you? Did you ever have an affair with your teacher and get dumped?

LAUREN. No.

DAZ. Well, don't tell me how I'm fucking feeling.

LAUREN. I'm still with mine.

DAZ. What?

LAUREN. Chris.

DAZ. Your teacher?

LAUREN. Swimming coach.

DAZ. Chris was your swimming coach?

LAUREN. When I was thirteen.

DAZ. Thirteen? A fuckin' paedo?

LAUREN. We didn't… not until… he encouraged me.

DAZ. What with? The breast stroke?

LAUREN. I knew you wouldn't understand.

DAZ. Oh, I get it alright.

LAUREN. I didn't want to talk about him. When I was with you, I wanted it to be our time.

DAZ. It was.

LAUREN. Not about him.

DAZ. Just us.

LAUREN. By ourselves.

DAZ. It still could be.

LAUREN. No, Daz.

DAZ. Why not?

LAUREN. Because I'm nearly thirty and you're…

DAZ. You said age doesn't matter.

LAUREN *is stumped*.

And you're right. I see it in me mam's magazines all the time. That Sadie Frost, she's always knocking off young lads and she's ancient.

LAUREN. Thanks.

DAZ. And that old fella… Michael Douglas. He married someone young enough to be his daughter.

LAUREN. They're not teachers!

DAZ. I'll be leaving school soon.

LAUREN. It…

DAZ. Then we can be together, do anything we like. We could run away.

LAUREN. Where would we go?

DAZ. Anywhere.

LAUREN. What would we live on?

DAZ. I've got four hundred pounds in me post-office savings.

   We'd be happy.

LAUREN. For how long?

DAZ. For ever.

LAUREN. That's a long time, Daz. I'll be a wrinkly old
   woman, and you'll be back with Sam Wright by then.

DAZ. She hasn't got a car.

LAUREN. Always the joker.

DAZ. Not any more.

LAUREN. Do you know how long we've spent in each other's
   company? I added it up, all those lunch hours.

DAZ. I don't care.

LAUREN. Before this weekend, not including teaching time.
   Two-and-a-half days. Two-and-a-half days, Daz.

DAZ. So.

LAUREN. The sum total of our relationship.

DAZ. It was a great two-and-a-half days.

LAUREN. I've known Chris for over sixteen years.

DAZ. That's…

LAUREN. A lifetime.

DAZ (*beat*). 'Five minutes of something wonderful, is better
   than a lifetime of nothing special.'

LAUREN. Profound.

DAZ. *Mystic Pizza*.

LAUREN. You've lost me.

DAZ. Me mam's favorite film.

LAUREN. Five minutes isn't enough, Daz.

DAZ. How about a lifetime? I don't care about anyone else, all I know is that I love you and I know that you love me. I know you haven't said it 'cos you're scared and I don't think I knew myself properly until this weekend. I know I've been in a strop, but I'll change. You're different from… you're sexy, good-looking, dead clever, you've got the best smile in the whole school and I don't want to lose –

LAUREN. We're getting married.

DAZ. Married?

LAUREN. Next month.

DAZ (*stunned*). I can't…

LAUREN. In the Dominican Republic.

DAZ. Why…

LAUREN. I couldn't…

DAZ. You can't.

LAUREN. It's booked.

DAZ. You came here knowing…

LAUREN. He booked it, a surprise.

DAZ. Don't let him bully you.

LAUREN. I'm not.

DAZ. You're going through with it?

LAUREN. It's for the best.

DAZ. Best for who?

LAUREN. For all of us.

DAZ. I won't let you.

LAUREN. You can't stop me.

DAZ. Wanna bet?

He picks up his phone.

LAUREN. Darren.

DAZ. These photos could be all round school, first thing
tomorrow morning. Wedding off.

LAUREN. You wouldn't.

DAZ. Try me.

LAUREN. You couldn't.

DAZ. Are you sure?

LAUREN. Yes.

DAZ. Is that your final answer?

LAUREN. I've deleted them.

DAZ. You've what?

LAUREN. If anyone saw them.

DAZ. They were all I had.

LAUREN. I'm sorry.

DAZ. I can't believe you deleted... us. I bet you've got photos
of him.

LAUREN. I'm not –

DAZ. Has he got a beard?

LAUREN. Honestly –

DAZ. I bet he smokes a pipe as well.

LAUREN. This is... please...

DAZ. Is that why you went for me, fancied a change? Wanted
some fresh-smelling smooth skin against yours?

LAUREN. Just shut up.

DAZ. Shut up? Don't tell me to shut up. You're not my
fucking mother.

LAUREN. I'm old enough to be.

Silence.

DAZ. What's his name?

LAUREN. You know it… Chris.

DAZ. Surname.

LAUREN. What's the –

DAZ. I want to know.

LAUREN. You'll laugh.

DAZ. I bet I fuckin' don't.

LAUREN (*beat*). McLeod.

DAZ. McLeod? (*Beat*.) Tell me, why do you move so fast? (*Beat*.) Do you love him?

LAUREN. He loves me.

DAZ. Do you love him?

LAUREN. Sort of.

DAZ. Sort of?

LAUREN. Darren.

DAZ. Does he know you 'sort-of' love him? Does he know the woman he's going to marry 'sort-of' loves him?

LAUREN. Stop it.

DAZ. I feel sorry for him, he hasn't got a clue what you are.

LAUREN. I just wanted some fun.

DAZ. Fun!

LAUREN. You don't realise how lucky you are.

DAZ. Lucky?

LAUREN. Hanging out with your mates, having a laugh. I never had that. While everyone else was drinking cider at the bus stop, I was doing a hundred lengths of the pool. Up at five every morning, weekends as well. Each night after school, head down, stay focused – I never had a chance to enjoy myself. Everyone in my class was living *Grange Hill* and I hadn't even seen it. I was never a teenager.

DAZ. You used me.

LAUREN. No.

DAZ. And now you're –

LAUREN. I'm doing this for you.

DAZ. Bollocks!

LAUREN. It's in your best interest.

DAZ. To lead me on? To flirt –

LAUREN. You made the first move.

DAZ. I wanted you.

LAUREN. You should be with someone your own age.

DAZ. I could have any lass in my year. But that night at Derwent Hill…

LAUREN. Not exactly Paris.

DAZ. It was for me.

LAUREN. I should have walked away.

DAZ. Why didn't you?

LAUREN. You can't swim against the tide.

DAZ. Did you ever feel –

LAUREN. 'Course I did.

DAZ. Not like me. I'm just a daft lad…

LAUREN. Don't, Darren.

DAZ. A stupid schoolboy with a silly crush.

LAUREN. No.

DAZ. And you just used me.

LAUREN. I love you.

DAZ (*beat*). Marry me.

LAUREN. What…

DAZ. We could…

LAUREN. I'd lose my job.

DAZ. I'm old enough.

LAUREN. That's not the point.

DAZ. Isn't it? Funny though, I turn sixteen and you –

LAUREN. Don't be ridiculous.

DAZ. You say you love me, but won't marry me. You're going to marry him, but you don't love him. I don't understand. My head's fucking banging.

LAUREN. You need to calm down.

DAZ. I want to go home.

LAUREN. Not like this.

DAZ. Are you going to take me?

LAUREN. Your mam's not expecting you until seven.

DAZ. Well, you could always phone her again and tell her we're coming home early, couldn't you 'Mrs *Greaves*'.

LAUREN. I can't believe I pretended.

DAZ. Well, you did.

LAUREN. For your birthday.

DAZ. Some present! You can't keep me here.

LAUREN. I'm not.

DAZ. I want to go home. Now.

LAUREN. When you calm down.

DAZ. This is kidnap.

LAUREN. Don't be so…

DAZ. I'm fucking out of here.

LAUREN. I can't let you leave.

DAZ. You've got no choice.

LAUREN. Not like this. Please, Daz, don't, I'm begging you.

Sit down, please.

DAZ *sits down*.

Thanks.

DAZ. I can't leave.

LAUREN. I can't change my mind.

DAZ. I know.

LAUREN. Then why stay?

DAZ. I haven't got me bus fare home.

LAUREN. Right.

DAZ. It's Sunday service.

LAUREN. I've always hated Sundays…

DAZ. Me too…

LAUREN. That sick feeling, that…

DAZ. I haven't done me homework…

LAUREN. Feeling. The end of…

DAZ. I can't believe this is it…

LAUREN. Over before it's…

DAZ. Game over.

LAUREN. Begun.

DAZ. We should have –

LAUREN. Swum against the tide.

DAZ (*beat*). I can't swim.

LAUREN. But you… you lied.

DAZ. You're the liar, I just can't crawl.

LAUREN. I would have taught you, I would have…

DAZ. Thrown me in the deep end.

LAUREN. Saved you.

DAZ. I need some air… this room…

LAUREN. It's changed.

DAZ. We've… I need to get out.

LAUREN. Calm…

DAZ. I'm sick of talking.

LAUREN. Hold on…

DAZ. Every man for himself.

I want to go home.

LAUREN. I need to know…

DAZ. You think I'd tell? Your secret's safe with me – memory deleted.

LAUREN. Memory deleted.

Lights fade.

End of Part One.

PART TWO

Scene One

Friday.

BETH *and* AIDEN *are in bed. A single red rose stands in an improvised vase – a plastic bottle. Next to it sits a cheap teddy bear clutching a heart on which 'I love Scarborough' is written. An iPod blares music.* BETH *and* AIDEN *get ready to hit the town. They drink alcopops.*

BETH. Lock up your sons, Beth is in town.

AIDEN. Shall we go to the same place as before?

BETH. Let's try somewhere on the front.

AIDEN. It's a bit tacky.

BETH. I'll show you tacky.

   BETH *gets out her phone and starts to show him photos of their last visit.*

AIDEN. Look at the state of me.

BETH. You look great.

AIDEN. With candyfloss all over my face? I'd forgotten about those hats.

BETH. I've still got mine.

AIDEN. I told you it rained that day.

BETH. It was just a few clouds. Anyway – (*She starts to make a move.*) the last thing on my mind's the weather.

AIDEN. Again? We've got all weekend for that.

BETH. Get in.

AIDEN. I'm sure the landlady suspects…

BETH. Nosy cow. (*Beat.*) I'll give her something to gossip about.

BETH bounces on the bed, making it creak, as if having sex.

AIDEN. Stop it.

BETH. I'm a naughty girl, spank me –

AIDEN. Beth!

AIDEN dives on her, trying to stop the noise, he holds his hand across her mouth. BETH is trying to say something but he can't make it out.

Promise you won't shout.

BETH. Mmm-mmm.

He removes his hand.

You're smothering me.

AIDEN. Are you saying I'm fat?

BETH. Cuddly.

AIDEN. I'll have you know I was regional under-eighteens swimming champion.

BETH. That was a while ago.

AIDEN. You cheeky bastard.

BETH. Joke, joke.

AIDEN. Not funny.

BETH. You're not fat.

Beat. AIDEN is still huffed.

You're not fucking fat.

Trying a different tactic, BETH picks up the bear and starts talking to him through it.

What are you doing, Daddy?

AIDEN *looks at her, he is playing unimpressed.*

Are you in a huff? Beth says she's really sorry.

AIDEN. Well, tell Beth, if she's really sorry she could tidy up her mess and unpack the rest of her stuff before we go out.

BETH. Beth says that's boring.

AIDEN. Life can be boring.

BETH. You look… mm-mmm… very sexy.

AIDEN. Do you think it's too much?

BETH. Yes. It's great. The more chest the better, I want to show you off to the world.

AIDEN. I need the…

He indicates to the bathroom.

BETH. Again?

AIDEN. It's those alcopops.

AIDEN *exits to the bathroom.* BETH *admires herself in the mirror, tests her breath against her hand.*

BETH (*to* AIDEN). Oh my God, it's happened again.

AIDEN (*offstage*). What?

BETH. Every time I look in the mirror, I get better looking. (*To* AIDEN.) Hurry up… (*To herself.*) You lucky lad… (*To* AIDEN.) Ha'way man, Aiden…

He enters.

AIDEN. I can't do it.

BETH. Do what?

AIDEN. I can't go out…

BETH. Are you okay?

AIDEN. Not really.

BETH. Are you sick?

AIDEN. Sort of.

BETH. It must be the WKD, I got them cheap from the dodgy offy, I bet they were out of date.

AIDEN. It's not the drink.

BETH. What then?

AIDEN. Someone might see us.

BETH. Aiden, lots of people are going to see us.

AIDEN. Exactly.

BETH. But they don't know who we are. They don't know...

AIDEN. I know.

BETH. So we'll steer clear of mind-readers.

AIDEN. I'm being serious. Anyone could see us.

BETH. We're not exactly the Beckhams, I don't think we're being tailed by the Geordie paparazzi.

AIDEN. I'm not going out.

BETH. Aiden, man.

AIDEN. I'm sorry, it's just...

BETH. It's me birthday tomorrow, we can't stay in all weekend.

AIDEN. I can't do it.

BETH. It didn't bother you last time.

AIDEN. That was just a day trip.

BETH. We played on the arcades, we went swimming.

AIDEN. I went swimming.

BETH. I forgot my kit. (*Beat.*) We even kissed in public.

AIDEN. It was dark.

BETH. Don't bullshit me, Aiden.

AIDEN. I'm the one taking all the risks. If we get found out…

BETH. We won't…

AIDEN. It's my life on the line. It's my…

BETH. Okay, okay, we'll stay in.

AIDEN. Thanks. (*Beat*.) I've got something that might cheer
you up.

He gets out her card and two presents, hiding the larger one.

BETH. It's not until tomorrow.

AIDEN. So!

BETH *starts to open the smaller present unenthusiastically.*

You're supposed to open the card first.

BETH. So!

It's a game for a PSP.

I haven't got a PSP.

AIDEN *reveals the larger present.*

No way.

AIDEN. Way.

She tears at the wrapping. It's a PSP. Clearly delighted.

BETH. Oh my God, this is the best present ever.

AIDEN. I'm glad you like it.

BETH. I fucking love it.

She gives him a big kiss.

Can I put it on?

AIDEN. Not now.

BETH. Wait till I tell Greavsie.

AIDEN. You can't say it was from me.

BETH. I'm not stupid.

AIDEN. I know, I just panic sometimes.

BETH. Well, you shouldn't.

AIDEN. I can't help it.

BETH. I've got a present for you.

AIDEN. For me?

BETH. To say thanks for this weekend.

AIDEN. You haven't opened your card yet.

BETH. Close your eyes.

AIDEN. Do I have –

BETH. Close them.

> AIDEN *closes his eyes.* BETH *takes out her school photo and puts it on the table.*

AIDEN. Can I open them?

BETH. Count to three.

AIDEN. One, two, three. (*He opens his eyes.*) Is this some kind of joke?

BETH. Do you not like it? Me mam says…

AIDEN. Beth, that's not the point. Where am I going to keep it?

BETH. In your office.

AIDEN. At school?

BETH. Unless you've got one somewhere else.

AIDEN. The same office I share with Mr Lynch? The same office I have tutorials in with your classmates?

BETH. I hadn't thought about that.

AIDEN. No, Beth, you never do.

BETH. Sorry.

AIDEN. I'm always the one thinking…

BETH. Alright, man.

AIDEN. The one planning…

BETH. I get your point.

AIDEN. The one organising.

BETH. Stop it, man, you're doing me head in.

AIDEN. Keep your voice down.

BETH (*sarcastically*). Are you frightened you might get found out? Frightened that the landlady might hear? (*Beat. Seriously.*) I'm not bothered who knows, I'm not ashamed…

AIDEN. I'm sorry, Bethany. The photo's lovely, it's just…

BETH. You could keep it in your drawer.

AIDEN. What would be the point?

BETH. To look at.

AIDEN. I'm sick of hiding.

BETH. Well, don't.

AIDEN. If anyone found out…

BETH. I know, you could lose your job.

AIDEN. It's more serious than that. If the head, if anyone ever…

BETH. They won't.

> BETH *puts the photo back in her bag.* AIDEN *smiles weakly.* BETH *starts to kiss him.*

AIDEN. What do you think you're doing?

BETH. You might as well take advantage while you still can, I'll be legal tomorrow.

> *Lights fade.*

Scene Two

Saturday.

BETH *enters with a bag of provisions, she is really agitated.*

AIDEN. What's the matter?

BETH. I've got some really bad news.

AIDEN. Beth, what is it?

BETH. I've just bumped into Mr Scott.

AIDEN (*beat, shocked*). The head?

BETH. Walking down the street. What the fuck's he doing in Scarborough?

AIDEN. Did he see you?

BETH. He said hello, wanted to know what I was doing here.

AIDEN. What did you say?

BETH. I said I was here with friends. But the… the look he gave us.

AIDEN. What look? Like what? Do it.

BETH. Like… (*She demonstrates.*) I was on my way out of the newsagent and there he was, I just froze. I said, 'Hello Sir', and he just… the look he gave us… he knows…

AIDEN. He doesn't know!

BETH. I'm telling you…

AIDEN. He doesn't know. He can't.

BETH. He must…

AIDEN. Shut up.

BETH. He must know that I'm… (*Laughing.*) only joking.

The penny drops. AIDEN *doesn't know whether to laugh or cry.*

AIDEN. You fucking shit. You little shit.

AIDEN *is frustrated and embarrassed to have been taken in, but better this than the alternative.* BETH *is creased up, glad to have some fun back in the relationship.*

Oh God.

BETH. What would he be doing in Scarborough?

AIDEN. That is not funny.

BETH. I'm really sorry.

AIDEN. It's so not funny.

She continues to laugh.

Beth! It's not fucking funny.

BETH. Come here.

AIDEN. Get away.

BETH. Okay, I'm really sorry.

AIDEN. You're not sorry.

BETH. It was funny. It was… (*She cracks up laughing.*)

AIDEN. It's not funny.

She continues to laugh.

Bethany!

BETH. I'm sorry, I am sorry.

They both crack up.

Serious.

AIDEN. Oh God.

BETH (*trying to be serious*). It's a great day out there – sun's shining, birds are singing.

AIDEN. Headmaster's on the prowl.

BETH. You're not going to believe anything I ever say again, are you?

AIDEN. No.

BETH. No.

AIDEN (*taking the piss*). Nah.

BETH. Nah?

AIDEN (*emphatic*). Never.

BETH. What if I said I loved you? (*Beat.*) Would you believe that?

AIDEN. Stop being stupid.

BETH. I'm not being stupid.

AIDEN. Yes you are.

BETH. Maybe I am, but it doesn't mean I'm lying.

AIDEN. Can we change the subject?

BETH. Okay.

> BETH *goes to the window.*

> I got you a paper.

> *He takes a copy of the* Sun *out of the bag* BETH *brought in. He looks disapproving.*

> I wanted to read the football.

AIDEN. I get enough sport at school.

BETH. Look at how fast those clouds are moving.

AIDEN. Yeah.

BETH. Why do clouds sometimes move fast and sometimes they don't move at all?

AIDEN. I don't know.

BETH. What's inside them?

AIDEN. Twenty questions!

BETH. It must be something inside them, or…

AIDEN. The wind.

BETH. Nah, too easy. Must be pressure, or atmosphere, or…

AIDEN. Why make it more complex than it is?

BETH. Scientific gas? Or it could be the amount of rain inside.

AIDEN. I don't know.

BETH. Well, you're the teacher.

AIDEN. PE teacher. You should take more notice in your geography class.

BETH. Why would I want to listen to Mrs Robson when I can watch you warming up in the yard.

AIDEN. One hundred lines – I must not perv on my teacher.

BETH. Doing your squat thrusts. I must have missed the introduction to clouds lesson.

AIDEN. Introduction to clouds. I'd like to introduce you to a cloud. Here's a cloud. Hello Mr Cloud.

BETH. Tell me, why do you move so fast?

They fall about laughing.

AIDEN. I wish we could just stay here for ever.

They have a moment.

BETH. What do you call the wife of a Scottish cloud?

AIDEN. I don't know, what do you call the wife of a Scottish cloud?

BETH. Mrs McCloud. I made that up. Do you get it?

AIDEN. Yes.

AIDEN *picks up the* Sun, *there is a paedophile story on the front page.*

BETH. What's up with you?

AIDEN. I can't believe you bought this shit.

BETH. I don't know what you want.

BETH *starts to read her magazine.*

AIDEN. Disgusting.

BETH. You don't have to read it.

AIDEN. I'm talking about the little kid who was molested.

BETH. Oh yeah – Pervert.

AIDEN. I mean, who could...

BETH. Fuckin' beast, they should lock him up and throw away the key.

AIDEN. Yeah.

They read for a while.

BETH. Have you ever thought of plastic surgery?

AIDEN. What are you saying?

BETH. Just asking.

AIDEN. Do you think I need it?

BETH. Loads of people are doing it.

AIDEN. You think I need it.

BETH. Well...

AIDEN. Don't you?

She looks pointedly at him.

BETH. A bit of enhancement wouldn't go amiss.

AIDEN. Fuck off.

BETH. Got ya!

AIDEN. Grow up.

BETH. You wouldn't fancy me then – Pervert!

AIDEN. Beth!

BETH. Cradle-snatcher!

AIDEN. You bastard!

BETH. Joke.

AIDEN. Not funny.

   BETH *blows him a kiss*.

   You think you're so clever.

BETH. I'm the teacher's pet.

   Something catches BETH*'s eye in the magazine,* AIDEN*'s interest is pricked. He surreptitiously looks over her shoulder.*

AIDEN. Like blonds, do you?

BETH. Who doesn't?

AIDEN. Young ones?

BETH. I'm sixteen.

   BETH*'s phone beeps, she has a text. She laughs.*

AIDEN. What's the big joke?

BETH. You wouldn't get it.

AIDEN. Is it from Sam?

BETH. Sam?

AIDEN. Forgotten him already?

BETH. I know who he is.

AIDEN. Did you buy him roses?

BETH. No.

AIDEN. I bet you did. Have you got photos of him on your phone?

BETH. No.

BETH *puts the phone in her pocket – guilty as charged.*

AIDEN. Do you still see him?

BETH. We're in the same year.

AIDEN. I meant…

BETH. I know.

AIDEN. Well?

BETH. Not really.

AIDEN. What's that supposed to mean?

BETH. Why are you so interested?

AIDEN. I'm not.

BETH. Well, can we drop it.

AIDEN. Please yourself.

BETH. Hang on, you're not…

AIDEN. No!

BETH. You are.

AIDEN. Don't be ridiculous.

BETH. Jealous.

AIDEN. Of a fifteen-year-old?

BETH. You've shagged one, why can't you be jealous of one?

Silence.

Anyway, you're the one with the girlfriend.

AIDEN. You're so immature.

BETH. Er – yes. What did you expect? Demi fucking Moore?

Long pause.

AIDEN. Do you ever think about the future?

BETH. What, like flying cars?

AIDEN. I'm being serious.

BETH. Me too, they'd be great. (*Beat.*) 'Course I think about the future. I want to get me A-levels and that, and maybe go to college, like you.

AIDEN. That's… great.

BETH. I don't want to end up like my mam and dad.

AIDEN. Not all marriages are bad.

BETH. How would you know?

AIDEN. Well, they can't be.

BETH. Don't see the point of marriage.

AIDEN. Why?

BETH. How many happily married couples do you know?

AIDEN. Lots.

BETH. Name one.

AIDEN. What?

BETH. Name one. 'Cos I don't know any.

AIDEN. That's because you're fifteen.

BETH. Sixteen. Prove me wrong.

AIDEN. You're putting me on the spot.

BETH. You said you knew loads.

AIDEN. Your mam and dad can't be that unhappy.

BETH. Can't stand each other.

AIDEN. They're still together.

BETH. He's a womanising bastard and she hates his guts.

AIDEN. Why don't they split up?

BETH. I don't know.

AIDEN. I suppose people have their reasons.

BETH. Stupid ones if you ask me. If you're that unhappy that you'd shag someone else, then why stay with the person in the first place?

AIDEN. Well, it's not as simple as –

BETH. It's black and white as far as I'm concerned. He's a bastard. He can get away with it so he does. He doesn't respect her, how can he? If you don't have respect…

She realises the implication of what she has just said.

AIDEN. Then what's the point.

BETH. Sorry, I…

AIDEN. Don't be.

BETH. I meant what I said.

AIDEN. Apology accepted.

BETH. When I said I loved you.

AIDEN. Beth.

BETH. For real… (*Long pause.*) Do you love me?

Lights fade.

Scene Three

Sunday.

AIDEN *is in the bathroom, finishing off a call to Chris.*

AIDEN (*offstage*). Still hungover... I know, sorry, we've been busy... yes, I've thought about it... we'll talk when I get back... yes, I miss you... okay, babe, bye... love you too. (*Kisses into phone and ends call.*)

AIDEN *enters.*

You were up early.

BETH. Couldn't sleep.

AIDEN. Where've you been?

BETH. Walking.

AIDEN. Obviously.

BETH. And thinking.

BETH *picks up the PSP and starts playing.*

AIDEN. We need to talk.

BETH. Shit.

AIDEN. Bethany.

BETH. Nearly got blasted.

AIDEN. Are you listening?

BETH. Yes. Get in.

AIDEN. This is serious.

BETH. I know, I'm onto my last life.

AIDEN. You've been playing all weekend.

BETH. Fuck. Game over. Must try harder.

AIDEN. We need to talk.

BETH. That's what they say in the films, when they're about to dump somebody.

AIDEN. Don't be unreasonable.

BETH. Unreasonable? I couldn't get a word out of you last night. Now you want to talk, so we'll talk. Fire away.

AIDEN. It's not…

BETH. Not what?

AIDEN. Well…

BETH. The same?

AIDEN. Working. It's not…

BETH. Funny that. It was working on Friday. 'Yes, Beth; more, Beth; I've never felt like this, Beth.'

AIDEN. I'm sorry, I thought…

BETH. Come on, don't be shy, Mr Potts, what were you thinking? You bring me here for a dirty weekend, a birthday treat. Then you go all weird on me. Won't go out. I'd like to know what the fuck's going on 'cos this is doing my head in.

AIDEN. This is really difficult for me.

BETH. Like Pythagoras.

AIDEN. I wish there was a formula.

BETH. Formula. I'll give you a formula. Beth, plus Aiden, to the power of Chris, equals Beth is fucked.

AIDEN. Don't bring her into it.

BETH. So it's okay for you to nag me about my ex all weekend, but I can't mention your girlfriend's name – cool.

AIDEN. I was out of order, I should never…

BETH. What's she like?

AIDEN. Beth.

BETH. It's an easy question.

AIDEN. I don't…

BETH. Well, I do, what the fuck's she like? Is she like me? What's so funny?

AIDEN. Nothing.

BETH. How old is she? She's young, isn't she? How old?

AIDEN. Forty –

BETH (*incredulous*). Forty?

AIDEN. Seven.

BETH. Forty-seven? (*Beat.*) Forty-fucking-seven!

She'll soon be dead.

AIDEN. It's not important.

BETH. What? The age or her?

AIDEN. The age… her… both.

BETH. Well, leave her.

AIDEN. What?

BETH. If she's not important, then leave her.

AIDEN. That's not… It's not as simple as that.

BETH. It is to me.

AIDEN. You don't understand.

BETH. Because I'm just a kid?

AIDEN. I never said that.

BETH. I'm old enough to shag, but not old enough to understand. Explain. Go on, you're the teacher.

AIDEN. I'm sorry, Beth.

BETH. What for? For nagging? For taking me to bed? For being a selfish bastard?

AIDEN. Please.

BETH. For breaking my...

AIDEN. Beth, don't...

BETH. Don't tell me what to do, we're not in school now.

AIDEN. I know how you must be feeling.

BETH. Do you? Did you ever have an affair with your teacher and get dumped?

AIDEN. No.

BETH. Well, don't tell me how I'm fucking feeling.

AIDEN. I'm still with mine.

BETH. What?

AIDEN. Chris.

BETH. Your teacher?

AIDEN. Swimming coach.

BETH. Chris was your swimming coach?

AIDEN. When I was thirteen.

BETH. Thirteen? A fuckin' paedo?

AIDEN. We didn't... not until... she encouraged me.

BETH. What with? The breast stroke?

AIDEN. I knew you wouldn't understand.

BETH. Oh, I get it alright.

AIDEN. I didn't want to talk about her. When I was with you, I wanted it to be our time.

BETH. It was.

AIDEN. Not about her.

BETH. Just us.

AIDEN. By ourselves.

BETH. It still could be.

AIDEN. No, Beth.

BETH. Why not?

AIDEN. Because I'm nearly thirty and you're…

BETH. You said age doesn't matter.

AIDEN *is stumped*.

And you're right. I see it in me mam's magazines all the time. That Sadie Frost, she's always knocking off young lads and she's ancient.

AIDEN. Thanks.

BETH. And that old fella… Michael Douglas. He married someone young enough to be his daughter.

AIDEN. They're not teachers!

BETH. I'll be leaving school soon.

AIDEN. It…

BETH. Then we can be together, do anything we like. We could run away.

AIDEN. Where would we go?

BETH. Anywhere.

AIDEN. What would we live on?

BETH. I've got four hundred pounds in me post-office savings.

We'd be happy.

AIDEN. For how long?

BETH. For ever.

AIDEN. That's a long time, Beth. I'll be a wrinkly old man, and you'll be back with Sam Wright by then.

BETH. He hasn't got a car.

AIDEN. Always the joker.

BETH. Not any more.

AIDEN. Do you know how long we've spent in each other's company? I added it up, all those lunch hours.

BETH. I don't care.

AIDEN. Before this weekend, not including teaching time. Two-and-a-half days. Two-and-a-half days, Beth.

BETH. So.

AIDEN. The sum total of our relationship.

BETH. It was a great two-and-a-half days.

AIDEN. I've known Chris for over sixteen years.

BETH. That's…

AIDEN. A lifetime.

BETH (*beat*). 'Five minutes of something wonderful, is better than a lifetime of nothing special.'

AIDEN. Profound.

BETH. *Mystic Pizza*.

AIDEN. You've lost me.

BETH. Me mam's favorite film.

AIDEN. Five minutes isn't enough, Beth.

BETH. How about a lifetime? I don't care about anyone else, all I know is that I love you and I know that you love me. I know you haven't said it 'cos you're scared and I don't think I knew myself properly until this weekend. I know I've been

in a strop, but I'll change. You're different from… you're
sexy, good-looking, dead clever, you've got the best smile in
the whole school and I don't want to lose –

AIDEN. We're getting married.

BETH. Married?

AIDEN. Next month.

BETH (*stunned*). I can't…

AIDEN. In the Dominican Republic.

BETH. Why…

AIDEN. I couldn't…

BETH. You can't.

AIDEN. It's booked.

BETH. You came here knowing…

AIDEN. She booked it, a surprise.

BETH. Don't let her bully you.

AIDEN. I'm not.

BETH. You're going through with it?

AIDEN. It's for the best.

BETH. Best for who?

AIDEN. For all of us.

BETH. I won't let you.

AIDEN. You can't stop me.

BETH. Wanna bet?

She picks up her phone.

AIDEN. Bethany.

BETH. These photos could be all round school, first thing
tomorrow morning. Wedding off.

AIDEN. You wouldn't.

BETH. Try me.

AIDEN. You couldn't.

BETH. Are you sure?

AIDEN. Yes.

BETH. Is that your final answer?

AIDEN. I've deleted them.

BETH. You've what?

AIDEN. If anyone saw them.

BETH. They were all I had.

AIDEN. I'm sorry.

BETH. I can't believe you deleted... us. I bet you've got photos of her.

AIDEN. I'm not –

BETH. Has she got a beard?

AIDEN. Honestly –

BETH. I bet she smokes a pipe as well.

AIDEN. This is... please...

BETH. Is that why you went for me, fancied a change? Wanted some fresh-smelling smooth skin against yours?

AIDEN. Just shut up.

BETH. Shut up? Don't tell me to shut up. You're not my fucking dad.

AIDEN. I'm old enough to be.

Silence.

BETH. What's her name?

AIDEN. You know it... Chris.

BETH. Surname.

AIDEN. What's the –

BETH. I want to know.

AIDEN. You'll laugh.

BETH. I bet I fucking don't.

AIDEN (*beat*). McLeod.

BETH. McLeod? (*Beat.*) Tell me, why do you move so fast? (*Beat.*) Do you love her?

AIDEN. She loves me.

BETH. Do you love her?

AIDEN. Sort of.

BETH. Sort of?

AIDEN. Bethany.

BETH. Does she know you 'sort-of' love her? Does she know the man she's going to marry 'sort-of' loves her?

AIDEN. Stop it.

BETH. I feel sorry for her, she hasn't got a clue what you are.

AIDEN. I just wanted some fun.

BETH. Fun!

AIDEN. You don't realise how lucky you are.

BETH. Lucky?

AIDEN. Hanging out with your mates, having a laugh. I never had that. While everyone else was drinking cider at the bus stop, I was doing a hundred lengths of the pool. Up at five every morning, weekends as well. Each night after school, head down, stay focused – I never had a chance to enjoy myself. Everyone in my class was living *Grange Hill* and I hadn't even seen it. I was never a teenager.

BETH. You used me.

AIDEN. No.

BETH. And now you're –

AIDEN. I'm doing this for you.

BETH. Bollocks!

AIDEN. It's in your best interest.

BETH. To lead me on? To flirt –

AIDEN. You made the first move.

BETH. I wanted you.

AIDEN. You should be with someone your own age.

BETH. I could have any lad in my year. But that night at Derwent Hill…

AIDEN. Not exactly Paris.

BETH. It was for me.

AIDEN. I should have walked away.

BETH. Why didn't you?

AIDEN. You can't swim against the tide.

BETH. Did you ever feel –

AIDEN. 'Course I did.

BETH. Not like me. I'm just a daft lass…

AIDEN. Don't, Bethany.

BETH. A stupid schoolgirl with a silly crush.

AIDEN. No.

BETH. And you just used me.

AIDEN. I love you.

BETH (*beat*). Marry me.

AIDEN. What…

BETH. We could…

AIDEN. I'd lose my job.

BETH. I'm old enough.

AIDEN. That's not the point.

BETH. Isn't it? Funny though, I turn sixteen and you –

AIDEN. Don't be ridiculous.

BETH. You say you love me, but won't marry me. You're going to marry her, but you don't love her. I don't understand. My head's fucking banging.

AIDEN. You need to calm down.

BETH. I want to go home.

AIDEN. Not like this.

BETH. Are you going to take me?

AIDEN. Your mam's not expecting you until seven.

BETH. Well, you could always phone her again and tell her we're coming home early, couldn't you 'Mr *Greaves*'.

AIDEN. I can't believe I pretended.

BETH. Well, you did.

AIDEN. For your birthday.

BETH. Some present! You can't keep me here.

AIDEN. I'm not.

BETH. I want to go home. Now.

AIDEN. When you calm down.

BETH. This is kidnap.

AIDEN. Don't be so…

BETH. I'm fucking out of here.

AIDEN. I can't let you leave.

BETH. You've got no choice.

AIDEN. Not like this. Please, Beth, don't, I'm begging you.

Sit down, please.

BETH *sits down*.

Thanks.

BETH. I can't leave.

AIDEN. I can't change my mind.

BETH. I know.

AIDEN. Then why stay?

BETH. I haven't got me bus fare home.

AIDEN. Right.

BETH. It's Sunday service.

AIDEN. I've always hated Sundays…

BETH. Me too…

AIDEN. That sick feeling, that…

BETH. I haven't done me homework…

AIDEN. Feeling. The end of…

BETH. I can't believe this is it…

AIDEN. Over before it's…

BETH. Game over.

AIDEN. Begun.

BETH. We should have –

AIDEN. Swum against the tide.

BETH (*beat*). I can't swim.

AIDEN. But you… you lied.

BETH. You're the liar, I just can't crawl.

AIDEN. I would have taught you, I would have...

BETH. Thrown me in the deep end.

AIDEN. Saved you.

BETH. I need some air... this room...

AIDEN. It's changed.

BETH. We've... I need to get out.

AIDEN. Calm...

BETH. I'm sick of talking.

AIDEN. Hold on...

BETH. Every man for himself.

I want to go home.

AIDEN. I need to know...

BETH. You think I'd tell? Your secret's safe with me – memory deleted.

AIDEN. Memory deleted.

Lights fade.

The End.

Other Titles in the Series

Howard Brenton
BERLIN BERTIE
FAUST *after* Goethe
IN EXTREMIS
NEVER SO GOOD
PAUL

Anupama Chandrasekhar
FREE OUTGOING

Olivier Choiniére
BLISS *trans*. Churchill

Caryl Churchill
BLUE HEART
CHURCHILL PLAYS: THREE
CHURCHILL: SHORTS
CLOUD NINE
A DREAM PLAY *after* Strindberg
DRUNK ENOUGH TO SAY I LOVE YOU?
FAR AWAY
HOTEL
ICECREAM
LIGHT SHINING IN BUCKINGHAMSHIRE
MAD FOREST
A NUMBER
THE SKRIKER
THIS IS A CHAIR
THYESTES *after* Seneca
TRAPS

Lucinda Coxon
HAPPY NOW?

David Edgar
ALBERT SPEER
CONTINENTAL DIVIDE
EDGAR: SHORTS
PENTECOST
PLAYING WITH FIRE
THE PRISONER'S DILEMMA
THE SHAPE OF THE TABLE
TESTING THE ECHO
A TIME TO KEEP *with* Stephanie Dale

Debbie Tucker Green
BORN BAD
DIRTY BUTTERFLY
RANDOM
STONING MARY
TRADE & GENERATIONS

Mary Kelly & Maureen White
UNRAVELLING THE RIBBON

Fin Kennedy
HOW TO DISAPPEAR COMPLETELY AND NEVER BE FOUND
PROTECTION

Ayub Khan-Din
EAST IS EAST
LAST DANCE AT DUM DUM
NOTES ON FALLING LEAVES
RAFTA, RAFTA...

Tony Kushner
ANGELS IN AMERICA – PARTS ONE & TWO
CAROLINE, OR CHANGE
HOMEBODY/KABUL

Elizabeth Kuti
THE SIX-DAYS WORLD
THE SUGAR WIFE

Conor McPherson
DUBLIN CAROL
McPHERSON: FOUR PLAYS
McPHERSON PLAYS: TWO
PORT AUTHORITY
THE SEAFARER
SHINING CITY
THE WEIR

Dan Muirden
THE THINGS GOOD MEN DO

Bruce Norris
THE PAIN AND THE ITCH

Jack Thorne
STACY & FANNY AND FAGGOT
WHEN YOU CURE ME

Enda Walsh
BEDBOUND & MISTERMAN
DISCO PIGS & SUCKING DUBLIN
THE SMALL THINGS
THE WALWORTH FARCE

Nicholas Wright
CRESSIDA
HIS DARK MATERIALS *after* Pullman
MRS KLEIN
THE REPORTER
THERESE RAQUIN *after* Zola
VINCENT IN BRIXTON
WRIGHT: FIVE PLAYS

A Nick Hern Book

Scarborough first published in Great Britain in 2008 as a paperback original by Nick Hern Books Limited, 14 Larden Road, London W3 7ST, in association with the Royal Court Theatre, London

Scarborough copyright © 2008 Fiona Evans

Cover illustration by Felipe Alcada; designed by Feast Creative
Cover designed by Ned Hoste, 2H

Typeset by Nick Hern Books, London
Printed in the UK by CPI Bookmarque, Croydon CR0 4TD

A CIP catalogue record for this book is available from the British Library
ISBN 978 1 85459 545 4